My First Penguin Book

JENNY KELLETT

BELLANOVA

MELBOURNE · SOFIA · BERLIN

My name is...
. . . .

Hey there! I'm Pebbles the penguin.

Most penguins live in COLD places!

Can you find me in the snow?

But, not all penguins live in cold places! Some, like the **African penguin**, live in **warm places** like South Africa.

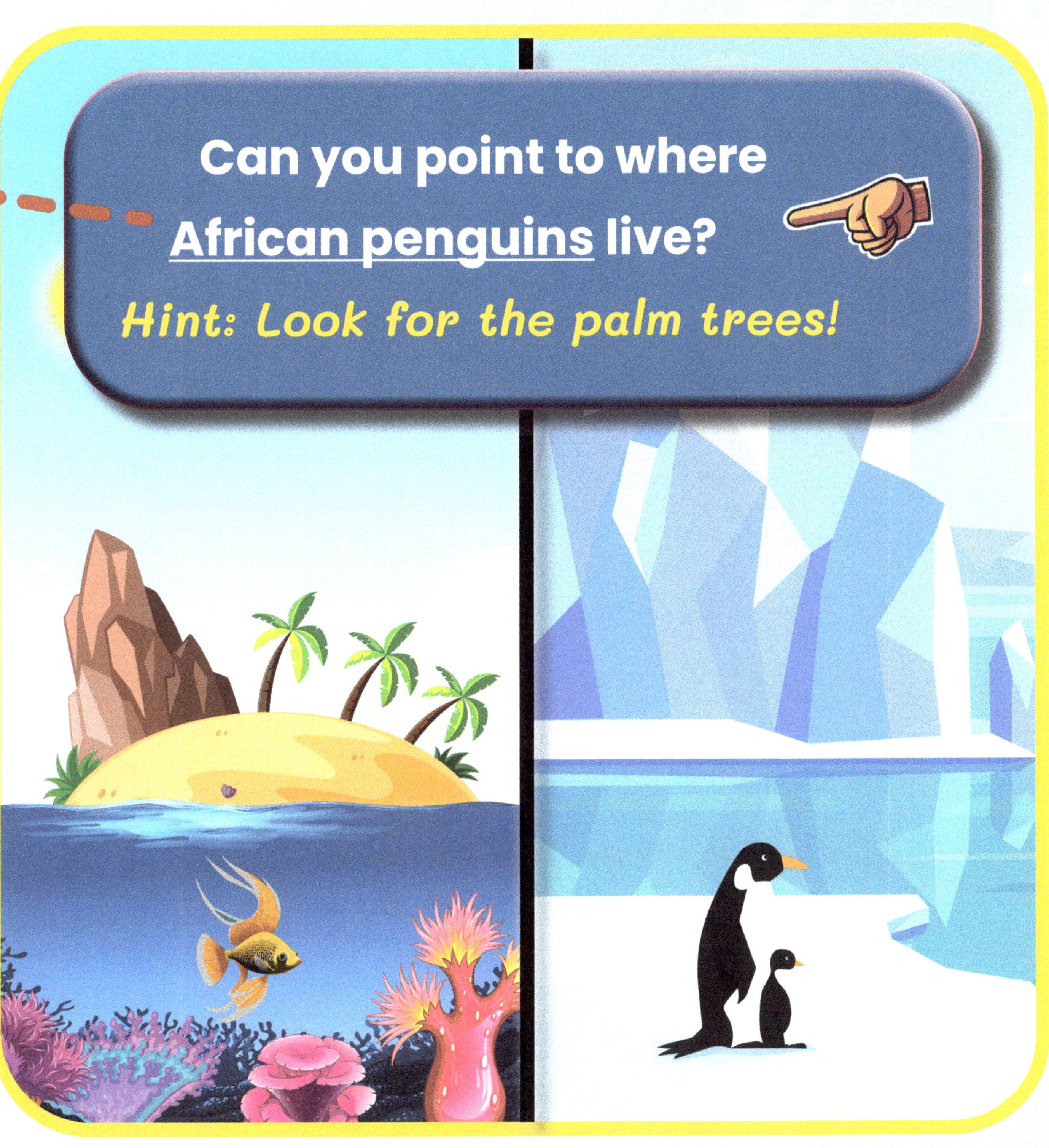

Can you point to where African penguins live?
Hint: Look for the palm trees!

Penguins waddle across the snow.

Can you waddle like a penguin?!

1 2 3 4
?
How many waddling
penguins can you count?

There are lots of different types of penguins!
I'm a rockhopper penguin!

Can you spot the
odd one out?

Which one is
not a penguin?

Penguins have wings, but they can't fly!

My ocean friends also love to swim!

Can you <u>match</u> them to their shadows?

Mmm, yummy!
Penguins love to eat fish!

Can you help me find some fish?

Point to all the fish you can see!

Baby penguins are called chicks.
They are small and very cute!

These animals also have chicks!

*Can you **match** these animals with their chicks?*

Chicken

Flamingo

Owl

Help Pebbles **find** her chick!

Trace the path with your finger that leads Pebbles to her chick.

Lookout for the walrus! 

Penguins have lots of friends!

My favorite activities....

Swimming

Hugging

Point to the pictures of
what **you** like to do with your friends!

Exploring

Playing

Chirp chirp!
Honk!
Squawk!
Penguins talk to each other using lots of different sounds!

Let's make some penguin sounds!
Chirp Chirp!
Honk!
Squawk!

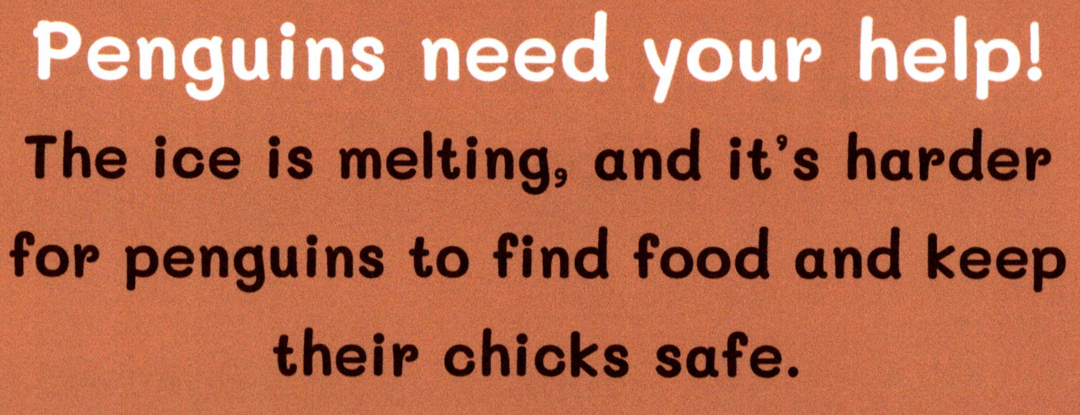

Penguins need your help!
The ice is melting, and it's harder
for penguins to find food and keep
their chicks safe.

You can help
them by taking
care of the
planet!

Penguins need clean oceans to stay safe

Trash can hurt penguins if they get tangled or eat it.

Help keep the oceans clean for penguins !
Which two items should go in the recycling bin?

What is your favorite thing about penguins?

What do penguins like to eat?

How can we help keep penguins safe?

Congratulations!

Name: ....

For learning all about

PENGUINS

And becoming a Certified Penguin Expert

Jenny Kellett
Author

ALSO BY JENNY KELLETT

Scan below to check out all our books!

Available at
www.bellanovabooks.com
and all major online bookstores.

We'd love to hear from you!

If you and your child enjoyed this book, we'd love to hear from you!

Leaving a **quick review** takes just a few seconds and makes a world of difference for us.

As an independent author, your support helps us create more fun and educational books. **Thank you!**

www.ingramcontent.com/pod-product-compliance
Lightning Source LLC
LaVergne TN
LVHW071747190726
843512LV00028B/1291